Rusick, Jessica,
Making With Metal : DIY
metalworking projects /
[2023]
33305257082119
ca   02/14/24

MAKING WITH METAL

DIY Metalworking Projects

Jessica Rusick and Ruthie Van Oosbree

Abdo & Daughters
MIDDLE GRADE NONFICTION
An imprint of Abdo Publishing
abdobooks.com

ABDOBOOKS.COM

Published by Abdo Publishing, a division of ABDO, PO Box 398166, Minneapolis, Minnesota 55439. Copyright © 2023 by Abdo Consulting Group, Inc. International copyrights reserved in all countries. No part of this book may be reproduced in any form without written permission from the publisher. Abdo & Daughters™ is a trademark and logo of Abdo Publishing.

Printed in the United States of America, North Mankato, Minnesota
102022
012023

THIS BOOK CONTAINS
RECYCLED MATERIALS

Design: Emily O'Malley, Mighty Media, Inc.
Production: Mighty Media, Inc.
Editor: Liz Salzmann
Projects: Tamara JM Peterson
Cover Photographs: Mighty Media, Inc. (front insets and phone stand), Nastya Sokolova/Shutterstock (back cover), Photographee.eu/Shutterstock (front background), tovovan/Shutterstock (phone screen)
Interior Photographs: iStockphoto, pp. 10 (bottom), 14 (left top), 17, 25 (bottom), 60 (top); MAURO CATEB/Flickr, p. 61 (bottom); Mighty Media, Inc., pp. 14 (top, right bottom), 24 (top left), 26, 28, 29, 30, 32, 33, 34, 36, 37, 38 (phone stand), 40, 41, 46–47, 48–49, 50–51, 52–53, 55 (top), 59 (top); Patrick McMullan/Getty Images, p. 59 (right bottom); Picasa/Wikimedia Commons, p. 9 (top); Shutterstock Images, pp. 3, 4, 5 (both), 6 (all), 8 (both), 9 (bottom), 11 (both), 12 (all), 13 (all), 14 (left middle, left bottom, right top), 15 (all), 16 (both), 18, 19, 20, 21 (both), 22 (all), 23 (all), 24 (top right, bottom left, bottom right), 25 (top left, top right), 38 (background, phone screen), 42, 44 (all), 45 (all), 54, 55 (bottom), 56, 57, 59 (left, right top), 60 (bottom), 61 (top); Wikimedia Commons, pp. 10 (top), 58
Design Elements: Mighty Media, Inc., Shutterstock

Library of Congress Control Number: 2021953166

PUBLISHER'S CATALOGING-IN-PUBLICATION DATA

Names: Rusick, Jessica and Van Oosbree, Ruthie, authors.
Title: Making with metal: DIY metalworking projects / by Jessica Rusick and Ruthie Van Oosbree
Other title: DIY metalworking projects
Description: Minneapolis, Minnesota : Abdo Publishing, 2023 | Series: Craft to career | Includes online resources and index.
Identifiers: ISBN 9781532198892 (lib. bdg.) | ISBN 9781098272821 (ebook)
Subjects: LCSH: Metal-work--Juvenile literature. | Metal sculpture--Juvenile literature. | Crafts (Handicrafts)--Juvenile literature. | Do-it-yourself products industry--Juvenile literature.
Classification: DDC 684.09--dc23

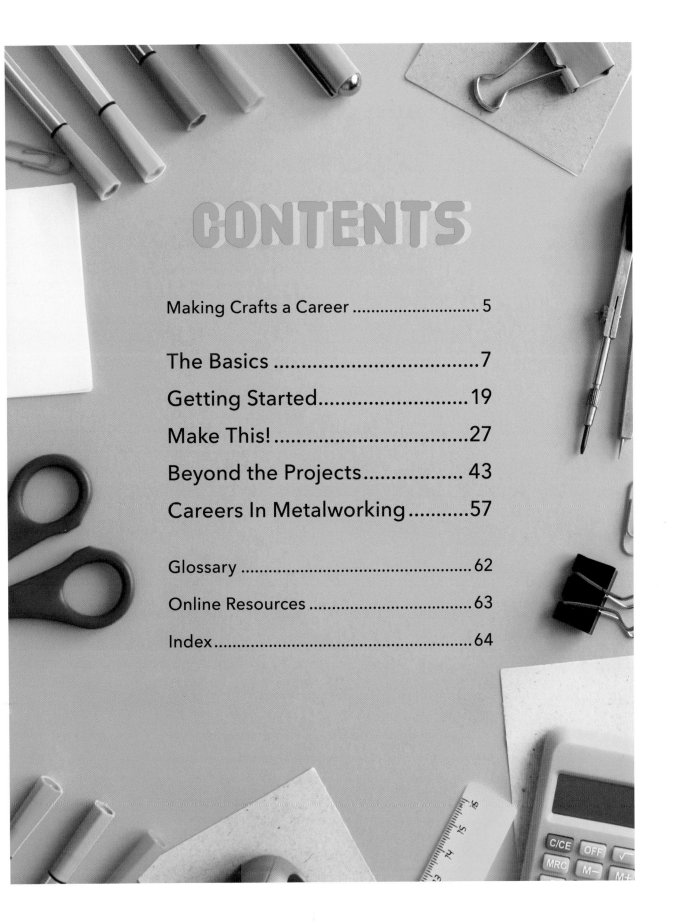

CONTENTS

MAKING CRAFTS A CAREER

What's your passion? Think about that hobby or activity that challenges, excites, and fulfills you—the one that makes you lose track of time. Maybe it's drawing, painting, sewing, or woodworking. Or perhaps there's something you've always wanted to try, like graphic design or metalworking.

Craftspeople make life more interesting. Their creations delight viewers while often serving a practical purpose. A well-crafted table is both useful and beautiful. A well-designed concert poster can draw fans in while providing important information. The details of a jacket or hat reflect an individual's personality and style.

Arts and crafts have been enriching the lives of artists and audiences for thousands of years. Many craftspeople have found ways to use their passion to support themselves financially, turning their craft into a career.

Anyone can become an artist. All you need is some basic knowledge, a little creativity, and a lot of patience. This book is full of tips, tricks, and techniques to get you started on the road from craft to career. What will you make?

Some metal products are made by melting the metal and pouring it into molds. This is called metal casting.

Most copper is mined using large, open-pit mines. Miners remove dirt and rock in layers to extract the copper.

Vases are often made out of metals such as brass or bronze, which don't rust.

WHAT IS METALWORKING?

Did you eat a meal with a stainless steel fork today? Did you lock your front door with a brass key? Are you wearing a gold or silver necklace? All these items were made with metalworking! Metalworking is shaping metal to make art or practical objects. You likely use objects that were made by metalworkers every day.

Metals come from the earth's crust. Some are elements, such as aluminum and gold. Other metals are alloys. An alloy is a mixture of a metal and at least one other element. Alloys may occur naturally. They can also be made by people.

Metals must be mined from underground. Some metals are found in ore. Ore is rock that contains metals or other valuable substances. After mining ore, people must smelt it or use other processes to remove the metal from the rock.

Some metals are very hard and durable. Alloys are often stronger than pure metals. Steel is a common example. It contains iron, a pure metal. Steel also contains carbon and other elements. These elements make steel stronger than iron alone. Steel is often used in construction because of its strength.

Other metals have different attributes that make them ideal for certain purposes. Aluminum is lightweight. It is often used in building airplanes, boats, and cars. Copper conducts heat and electricity well. It is often used in electrical wires. Because gold is so rare, it is used for money. Gold is also a soft, workable metal. This is one reason it's often included in alloys for making jewelry.

Human-made alloys are some of the most common metals used today. Scientists continue working to improve existing metals and develop new ones.

HISTORY OF METALWORKING

People have been metalworking for thousands of years. Gold, silver, and copper were some of the first metals people used. Around 3300 BCE, the Bronze Age began in the Middle East. This is when people started working with bronze and other alloys. They made tools, weapons, and art. They also began casting metal.

People traveled and traded metals. Different metalworking materials, techniques, and styles spread across cultures in this way. The Iron Age began around 1200 BCE. In the following centuries, people began using metal to make coins, armor, utensils, and more.

By the Middle Ages, which started in Europe around 500 CE, blacksmiths had become important members in communities. Blacksmiths shaped iron and steel into horseshoes and other everyday essentials.

Over time, metalworking techniques improved and new metals were discovered. Machines and methods of mass production also changed the metalworking industry. By the mid-1900s, most metalworking was done by machines. People began to view blacksmithing as an outdated occupation.

However, modern cultures still depend on metalworking. It is necessary for electronics, construction, and transportation. Other new technologies, such as laser cutting, artificial intelligence, and 3D printing, continue to change the metalworking industry.

In the Byzantine Empire, from about 400 to 1450 CE, people used various copper coins.

METALWORKING TIMELINE

8000 BCE

People in the Middle East are the first known to use copper.

3300–1200 BCE

The Bronze Age: Bronze replaces copper as the major material used in metalworking.

200 BCE

The Chinese start making steel.

1480

Leonardo da Vinci designs a machine that shapes lead for stained-glass windows. Machines based on his design were in use by the 1600s.

1856

Henry Bessemer patents the Bessemer process, which allows for the mass production of steel.

1900–TODAY

Metal is mass-produced for automobiles, construction, electronics, and more.

7000 BCE

Ancient Native American societies near the Great Lakes begin making copper tools.

1200 BCE–550 CE

The Iron Age: Iron replaces bronze as the major material using in metalworking.

476 CE–1400 CE

The Middle Ages: Metalworkers in Europe craft religious objects.

1825

Aluminum is first separated from ore. It eventually becomes a popular metalworking material.

1885

Czar Alexander III of Russia commissions the first Fabergé egg. These eggs were works of art crafted with gold and other precious metals, as well as gemstones.

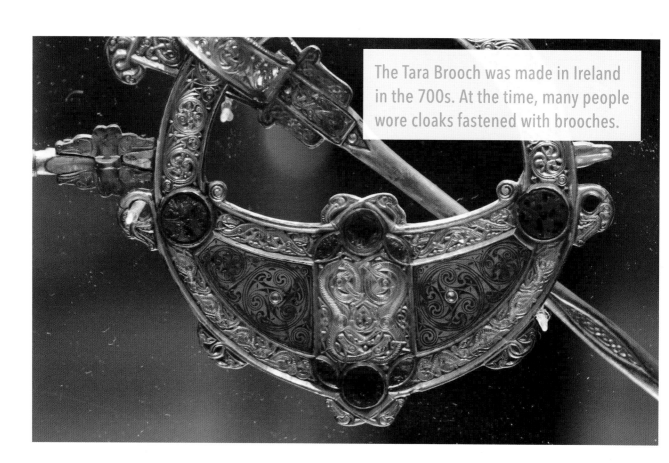

The Tara Brooch was made in Ireland in the 700s. At the time, many people wore cloaks fastened with brooches.

Gold is valued in many cultures. It has been associated with gods and included in legends and fairy tales. It is also a symbol of wealth, power, and immortality.

METALWORKING & CULTURE

Metalworking has been an essential part of human cultures since people first learned how to shape metal. Metalworking provides tools for farming, utensils for eating, and materials for building. It is also used to create religious objects, musical instruments, and art.

Today, most metalworking is done through manufacturing. But many individuals still work with metal as a hobby or for business. People use metal to both express themselves and to create useful items.

Metalworkers may learn their craft in classes they take through school or local studios. And the internet makes getting into metalworking even easier than before. Anyone can watch YouTube videos to learn metalworking techniques! Many tutorials and blogs about metalworking projects also exist. And many metal artists can sell their work on sites such as Etsy.

Interest in hobby metalworking has increased in recent years as more buyers want to purchase handmade and custom metal items. Some people are returning to blacksmithing. And the number of female blacksmiths has risen.

Interest in the hobby has also increased because of the COVID-19 pandemic. At the start of the pandemic in 2020, many people had more free time than ever before. Some used this time to try new crafts, including metalworking.

In Trinidad and Tobago, the steelpan has its roots in a long drumming tradition among people who came there from Africa.

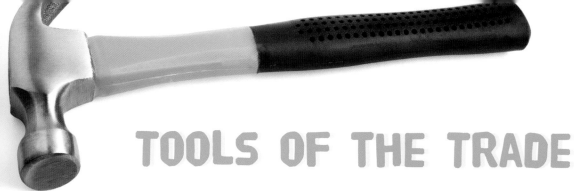

TOOLS OF THE TRADE

Here are some of the tools you will need as you dive into the world of metalworking.

BASIC ITEMS

METAL SHEETS

Aluminum, copper, brass, and other types of metal are sold in sheets. These sheets are made in a range of sizes and thicknesses. Thin sheets of metal can be cut and bent into different shapes.

SAFETY WARNING

The edges of metal sheets can be very sharp. Wear gloves and be careful when crafting with them.

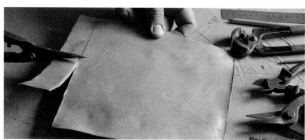

CUTTING TOOLS

Metalworking requires a variety of tools for cutting metals. Tin snips, or shears, are designed for cutting thin sheets of metal. Wire cutters are designed to cut metal wire. Both of these tools come in many different sizes, shapes, and strengths. If you're cutting foil, regular scissors will work.

METAL WIRE

Many metalworking projects use wire. It is an especially common tool in jewelry making. Metal wire is available in many thicknesses and ranges of flexibility.

PLIERS

Pliers can help bend and shape metal and wire. They can also hold pieces in place while you hammer or bend them with

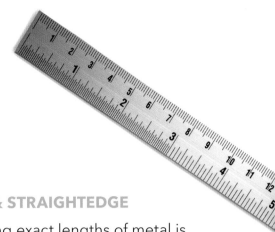

another tool. Needle-nose pliers have long jaws. The insides of the jaws are flat, making them great for holding things in place and bending thin metal. Round-nose pliers have rounded jaws. These are often used when shaping wire. Linesman's pliers are larger and stronger. They can be used to bend sheet metal.

HAMMER

A hammer can be used to aid in embossing, punching, and shaping metal. It is also used to insert nails into thin metal pieces.

PAINT

Acrylic paint and spray paint both work on metal. Paint is usually applied toward the end of a project, after the metal has been shaped.

RULER & STRAIGHTEDGE

Measuring exact lengths of metal is an essential part of some projects. So is cutting straight lines. Rulers and ruled straightedges can help with both of these tasks.

SPECIALTY TOOLS

The tools below will help you take your metalworking projects to the next level!

SOLDERING IRON

A soldering iron (SAH-dur-ing EYE-urn) is used to join two metal pieces together with a metal substance called solder. Always choose lead-free solder for your projects.

SAFETY WARNING

Soldering irons and solder get very hot. Always use them carefully and with adult supervision while wearing proper safety gear, such as gloves.

FLUX

Flux is brushed on metal surfaces to help solder bond to the surfaces. Always choose rosin-free flux.

FILES & SANDPAPER

Soldering and welding can leave behind rough edges. These edges can be smoothed with sandpaper or a file. There are flat and rounded files, as well as files with both flat and round sides or other features. A power tool called a die grinder can also smooth metal surfaces.

SPECIALTY GLUE

Regular glue often doesn't work well on metal. Special glue is necessary to glue metal pieces to each other or to other surfaces. Effective glues include epoxy glue, polyurethane glue, and super glue.

BEADS

Beads are great for jewelry making. They also add color and flair to other projects. Craft stores carry beads made of glass, plastic, metal, and other materials. Make sure to choose beads with holes large enough for any wire you plan to thread through them.

METAL HOLE PUNCH

Some projects require cutting holes in sheets of metal. This can be done most easily with a metal hole punch. Metal hole punches can be small handheld devices shaped like pliers. Others attach to tables and have an arm that moves up and down to punch holes.

STAMPS

Stamps have raised designs on them that can be pressed into metal. Some stamps made of metal can be hammered into a metal surface. This transfers the image onto the metal.

PATINA MIXTURE

Patina is a layer that naturally develops on copper or bronze as it ages. It is usually greenish in color. A patina can also be artificially added to metal. Certain mixtures, such as vinegar and sea salt, can be applied to these metals to create a patina within a few days.

HACKSAW

Some metal can't be cut with shears. Hacksaws are handheld saws that can cut through thick, strong metal. A hacksaw blade has small teeth. It is held in place by a rigid frame.

VISE

A vise attaches to a table or other work surface. It is used to hold metal in place while you work with it. Put a cloth between the vise and the metal to keep the metal from getting scratched.

EMBOSSING TOOLS

There are a few special tools designed for embossing thin sheets of metal. Rollers flatten the metal. Embossing sticks and styluses are used to gently push the metal into a raised position following a stencil or other design. A sheet of craft foam provides a soft surface for the stick or stylus to press the metal into.

MATERIALS MATTER

There are many types of metal to choose from in metalworking. Follow this quick guide to figure out which are best for your project.

	Cost (1–5, 5 most expensive)	Good for Soldering?	Flexibility
Aluminum	2	No	High
Brass	3	Yes	Medium
Bronze	4	Yes	Medium
Copper	5	Yes	High
Stainless Steel	1	No	Low

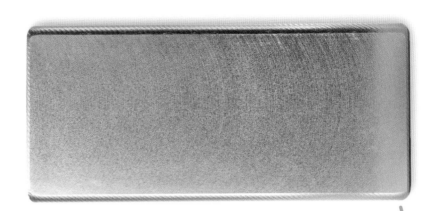

Advantages	Disadvantages
Lightweight. Available in many household items, such as soda cans and aluminum foil. Conducts heat and electricity well.	Not very strong. Corrodes when exposed to salt.
Shares many advantages of copper but is less expensive. Easy to cut. More bendable than bronze. Color can resemble gold.	Requires maintenance to prevent tarnish. Can crack if exposed to ammonia.
Shares many advantages of copper but is less expensive. Easy to cut. Stronger than copper and brass. Good for sculpture casting.	More brittle than copper and brass.
Patina helps it last longer and may be appreciated for appearance. Resists bacteria. Unique reddish-brown color.	Patina may not be desired. Scratches easily.
Resistant to rusting. Very strong. Durable.	Difficult to bend and shape without advanced machinery. Does not conduct heat and electricity well.

SETTING UP YOUR SHOP

Many craftspeople find they do their best work when they have a dedicated workspace. There, the materials they need are within arm's reach, and artists can let their creativity shine. Where will you set up your workshop?

A metalworking shop can be as big as a room or as small as a kitchen table. No matter where you decide to work, here are a few things to keep in mind:

> Make sure you have enough space to work and that the floor is clear of wires and any other tripping hazards.

> Choose a well-ventilated area for any activities that may produce fumes or dust, such as soldering and welding.

> You will want a large, clean, flat surface to work on. This could be a workbench or a sturdy table.

> There are many metalworking tools to choose from. Start with the most affordable and basic tools, which will mostly be manual hand tools.

> Make sure you have a safe, dry place to store your metals and works in progress.

MAKER TIP

Many metalworking tools and machines are too big, expensive, or dangerous for most people to own. But some cities have local workshops or studios where people can take classes, rent tools, or use heavy machinery. These can be a great option if you want to weld, cut thick metal, or use a tool that requires an experienced metalworker's training and supervision.

BE SMART WITH YOUR ART

Your shop is set up and you're ready to make! There are a few things to keep in mind as you begin your exploration of metalworking.

CHOOSE YOUR TOOLS WISELY. The right tools can make or break a project. Make sure all your tools are in good working order.

SAFETY FIRST. Many metalworking tools and materials are sharp. You are in charge of staying safe in your shop! Work carefully and slowly when using these tools. Read the instructions or get a lesson on using any tools unfamiliar to you before beginning a project.

TAKE YOUR TIME. Metalworking takes patience! Plan your project before beginning. Gather all the materials you need and research any new techniques you will be using. Prepare materials carefully. Then work slowly, especially when you are still mastering techniques.

PRACTICE, PRACTICE, PRACTICE! It's a good idea to try new techniques on scrap metal. If your scrap pieces are the same type of metal as a main project, you can also use them to test how easily the metal can be cut, bent, stamped, or soldered.

BE FLEXIBLE. Projects often don't go exactly as planned. That's part of the fun! Don't be afraid to change a material, technique, or even the original plan to solve a problem that comes up during your project. Your brain is your most important tool!

TIPS & TECHNIQUES

The more metalworking projects you do, the more you'll learn what materials and methods you like best. Here are a few tips and techniques to get you started.

EXPERIMENT WITH MATERIALS

Most craft stores carry affordable metal sheets, wire, and blanks. Buy some inexpensive materials to practice with. You might try different types of metal or different thicknesses. You can practice techniques for a project you're working on. Or you can try out a new technique you're just learning!

MEASURE & WORK SLOWLY

Some mistakes in metalworking may mean you have to start over. But there are ways to avoid these mistakes. As you work, have patience. Take time to measure and then double-check your measurements before cutting or joining pieces. Work slowly and complete project steps in order. But also, don't worry if you have to start over. It's an unavoidable part of many crafts.

TOOL CARE

Being knowledgeable about and responsible with your tools is essential in metalworking. Watch videos or read information about the proper use of tools. Read instruction manuals for power tools and check that they are in working condition before each use. Never use damaged, bent, or dull tools. Many hardware stores offer tool-sharpening services.

PREPARE FOR THE ELEMENTS

If your metalworking project will be kept outdoors, it's important to choose the right materials and protective products. Use metals that are resistant to rust, such as aluminum, copper, brass, bronze, and stainless steel. Use a paint that is designed for outdoor use. You may also wish to use a metal sealant, depending on your materials and climate.

TRY NEW TOOLS

As you become more comfortable with metalworking and using certain tools, you may wish to look into buying more advanced tools. These could include aviation snips, specialty hammers, and mallets made with materials that won't damage metal. There are also power tools available for cutting, rolling, and drilling metal.

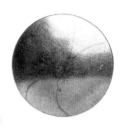

CHOOSING SUPPLIES

Purchasing metal for your project can be confusing. Metals come in many different forms. They are measured in different ways. Understanding what you're purchasing and why is important.

METAL SHEETS

Metal sheet thickness is measured by gauge. Different metals have different gauge measurement systems. So, two sheets of different metals that are the same thickness will have different gauges. Thicker sheets have lower gauge numbers. However, not all brands will give a gauge. They may indicate thickness in inches. Experiment with different metals and different thicknesses to become familiar with how they work. This will help you choose the right thickness for your projects.

METAL WIRE

Metal wire is also measured by gauge. Just as thinner sheets have higher gauge numbers, thinner wires have higher gauge numbers. Wire is also measured in hardness. Wire hardness can be very important. Wire can be dead soft, half-hard, or full-hard. Dead soft wire is easily bent but it may not hold its shape as well. Half-hard and hard wire will hold their shape better, but they are more difficult to shape.

METAL BLANKS

Metal blanks are designed for stamping. They are flat, shaped pieces of metal. They come in

many different sizes and types of metal. Softer metals are easier to stamp but may not be as durable. Common softer metals include aluminum, copper, and pewter. Harder metals are more resistant to scratches but are harder to stamp. Brass and sterling silver are two common harder metals.

FOILS & LEAF

Foils are very thin metal sheets. Aluminum and copper are commonly used in making foil. Silver and gold are sometimes used to make foil that is used for metal leaf. This is very thin foil that tears easily. It is meant to be put onto other surfaces, usually for decoration. Depending on the type of metal, foil can be expensive.

UPCYCLING

Upcycling is a great way to reduce waste and create practical or artistic objects. Finding metal to transform into something new is a fun challenge. Some materials,

such as aluminum cans and bottle caps, are probably in your recycling bin already. Other materials, such as old silverware, may not be as readily available. Look in antique and thrift stores for metals to upcycle. Be safe when working with any upcycled metal. It may be harder to cut and may have sharp edges. Some metals also may have harmful substances on them, so make sure your metal is clean before you start crafting. Use caution with rusty materials. These items may have rougher surfaces.

SUNCATCHER

Wire bending is a simple technique that can produce beautiful results. It has been an art form for thousands of years. It is often used to create jewelry and other decorative pieces. Use wire, pliers, and some colored beads to make an elegant suncatcher!

STUFF YOU NEED

safety goggles	beads	jump rings
thin wire	needle-nose pliers	thick wire
wire cutters	thick metal hanger	

2

3

TIP

When choosing beads, think about how they will look in the sun. For example, translucent beads with angular facets catch sunlight well.

1 Cut several different lengths of wire. The wire should be thin enough to thread through the beads, but thick enough to hold its shape.

2 String beads onto the wires. Use a needle-nose pliers to make loops at the top and bottom of the wires to secure the beads in place.

3 You can also use pliers to bend some wires into loops and spirals. Attach them to the beaded wires to make longer decorations.

4

6

4 Use pliers to take apart a thick metal hanger and bend it into a wavy pattern. Shape one portion into a loop for hanging.

5 Use jump rings to attach the wire pieces to the hanger.

6 To hang the suncatcher, attach a length of thick wire through the loop you made in step 4.

7 Hang the suncatcher outside or by a sunny window!

What else can you bend?
Find out how to make it your way on page 46!

LIZARD WALL ART

Metal cutting is an easy way to form shapes out of thin metal sheets. Punching and embossing can add details to cut shapes. Use these techniques to create lizard wall art!

STUFF YOU NEED

plain paper

pencil

protective gloves

thin aluminum sheet

tape

tin snips

pliers

craft foam

slotted screwdriver or stylus

hammer

metal hole punch (optional)

spray paint or acrylic paint and paintbrush

thin nails

piece of wood

1

2

TIP

Don't try to cut metal in a continuous line. Instead, cut away large areas and then cut smaller sections one at a time. To get into tight corners, cut from both directions.

1 Draw an outline of a lizard on a sheet of paper. Tape the drawing to the aluminum sheet.

2 Cut around the outline with tin snips. Be careful of the cut edges, as they can be sharp. Set aside any large scraps of metal to use later in the project. Remove the paper from the lizard cutout.

3 Gently bend down the edges of your lizard with pliers. This will create a 3D effect. Move around the lizard in one direction, trying to keep the bend even and continuous.

4 To give smaller pieces dimension, turn the lizard over and place it on a sheet of craft foam. Place the end of a slotted screwdriver or stylus in the area you need to form. Lightly tap the screwdriver or stylus with a hammer to raise, or emboss, the area.

3

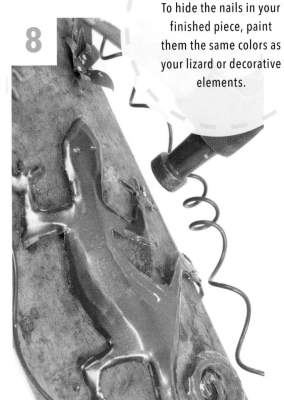

8

TIP

To hide the nails in your finished piece, paint them the same colors as your lizard or decorative elements.

5 If you'd like, use a metal hole punch to add eyes or other decorations to the lizard.

6 Use tin snips to create flowers, leaves, or other decorative elements using metal scraps from step 2.

7 Paint the lizard and decorations with spray paint or acrylic paint.

8 Use thin nails to attach the lizard and decorations to a piece of wood.

What else can you cut, punch, and emboss?
Find out how to make it your way on page 48!

GLASS LANTERN

Soldering is used to join two metal pieces together quickly and cleanly. Professional metalworkers solder electronics, jewelry, and more. Practice your soldering skills by making a gorgeous glass lantern!

STUFF YOU NEED

5 colored glass squares

colored glass beads

copper foil

safety goggles

protective gloves

face mask

flux

paintbrush

soldering iron and solder

battery-powered tea light

1

2

TIP

Use an additional glass square to add a top to your lantern. Only do this if you are using a battery-powered light. If you are using a candle, do not add a top to your lantern.

1 Cover the edges of the glass squares and beads with strips of copper foil.

2 Lay four of the glass squares in a row. They will be the sides of your lantern. Arrange beads along the top edge of each square.

3 Brush flux onto the copper foil around the beads and along the tops of the squares.

4 Solder the beads in place. Hold the soldering iron in your dominant hand and the roll of solder in your other hand. Carefully touch the two ends together and slowly run the solder and iron across the copper foil between the beads and glass squares. Make sure the solder covers the foil completely and evenly. If necessary, go back and fix any areas that need more solder.

4

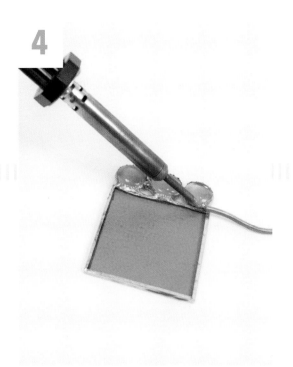

7

5 Carefully turn the glass squares over. Repeat step 4 to solder the opposite sides of the beads and squares.

6 Stand the side squares upright around the fifth square to form a box.

7 Use the technique in step 4 to join the squares by soldering the edges.

8 Place a battery-powered tealight inside the lantern and watch it glow!

What other metal projects can you solder?
Find out how to make it your way on page 50!

SILVERWARE PHONE STAND

Upcycling means turning old items into new products and works of art. You can upcycle metal to create furniture, accessories, and more. Try upcycling old silverware into a person-shaped cell phone stand!

STUFF YOU NEED

2 metal knives	3 metal spoons	towel
vise	water	epoxy
hammer or pliers	soap	masking tape or painter's tape

3

6

TIP

A thrift store is a great place to find cheap silverware to upcycle.

1. The two knives will be the stand's legs. Clamp the handles of the knives in the vise. Use a hammer or pliers to bend the tips of the knives 90 degrees to form feet.

2. Two spoons will be the stand's arms. Clamp the handles of these spoons in the vise. Bend the middle of each spoon 20 degrees to form elbows.

3. Clamp the bowl of one of the arm spoons in the vise. Bend the middle of the bowl 90 degrees to form a hand.

4. Repeat step 3 with the other arm spoon.

5. Wash and dry all the silverware.

6. Mix the epoxy according to the directions on the package. It will begin to cure within a few minutes, so be ready to use it quickly.

7. Use the epoxy to glue the top inner edges of the legs together.

8

TIP

Bend silverware in different ways to make additional stands for other items. Could you make a stand for glasses or jewelry?

10

8 The third spoon is the stand's body and head. Glue the joined legs behind the handle of this spoon. Use masking tape or painter's tape to hold the pieces together while the epoxy cures.

9 Glue the tops of the arms together in a V shape. Then glue the arms onto the back of the body, below the head. The arms should angle down so the hands are near the legs. Use masking tape or painter's tape to hold the pieces together.

10 After the epoxy cures, remove the tape. Then use your silverware sculpture as a cell phone stand!

MAKE IT YOUR WAY!

Following instructions to complete a specific project is a great way to learn and master new techniques. But now it's time to let your creativity shine. Design and create your own projects by mixing and matching the different techniques you learned in this book! Keep these tips in mind as you're planning and working on your project.

GET INSPIRED

Inspiration is all around you! The internet is full of tutorials, videos, and images that can give you project ideas and teach you new techniques. Metals come from the earth. Look at the colors and patterns of landforms and rocks to inspire your metalworking project. Explore the metalworking practices of your own and other cultures. And look at what metal items are popular in the stores you like. Then, think of ways you can put your own stamp on these projects.

USE WHAT YOU HAVE

Sometimes, tools you already have on hand can direct the project you will create. Do you have old silverware or jewelry that could be upcycled? Do you have leftover spray paint? Use it to decorate metal. And vinegar can help create an authentic-looking patina.

PROBLEM-SOLVE

Plans change! Materials run out! Techniques fail! Don't sweat your mistakes. Instead, look at them as opportunities to learn and grow. Sometimes, an unexpected issue might send your project in a new direction you never would have thought of. Be open and flexible, and you'll create a project that is unique and entirely *you*.

COLLABORATE

Stuck? Don't be afraid to ask for help! A classmate might bring a new perspective to your project. And a teacher or parent might know just how to solve the problem you're having. You can also seek expert advice online or from metalworking organizations in your area!

THE ELEMENTS OF DESIGN

Anytime you're planning a new metalworking project, consider the elements of design. These are the basic units of a visual image. There are many ways to approach these elements when imagining and creating.

FORM

This is the space a piece of art occupies. Form can be two-dimensional or three-dimensional.

LINE

A line is the connection between two points. Lines can be vertical, horizontal, diagonal, straight, or curved.

SHAPE

Shape is the outline of a certain area. A shape can be geometric, organic, or abstract.

SPACE

Positive space is the area that the subject of the art takes up. Negative space is the empty space around the subject. Artists use space to draw viewers' eyes to certain areas.

TEXTURE

This is the way an object feels or appears to feel. It can be soft, rough, smooth, fuzzy, and much more!

COLOR

Color is often used to convey the mood of a piece of art. Many designers use a color wheel to choose a color scheme for their work.

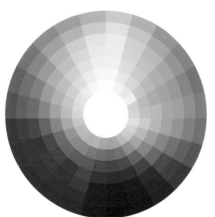

WIRE BENDING
& MORE

You can bend wire into almost any shape you can think of. This art form is perfect for creating jewelry and other decorative designs. What will you bend?

Use rounded needle-nose pliers to shape wire into loops, circles, and coils. Turn metal wire into jewelry, ornaments, sculptures, and more!

Make jewelry using wire, beads, and gems. Add jewelry findings such as clasps, earring wires, and pin backs to finish the pieces.

CUTTING, PUNCHING, EMBOSSING
& MORE

Add depth and details to your projects using cutting, punching, and embossing techniques. Adding a colorful patina to metal is also a great way to make your project stand out. What techniques will you use?

Try making a night-light by punching holes in a metal sheet or can and placing it in front of a light.

Ammonia or a salt-vinegar mixture can be used to create a patina on copper. Try different formulations to see which you like best. If using ammonia, make sure the area is well-ventilated and there's an adult supervising. Copper will also form a patina naturally if left outside.

49

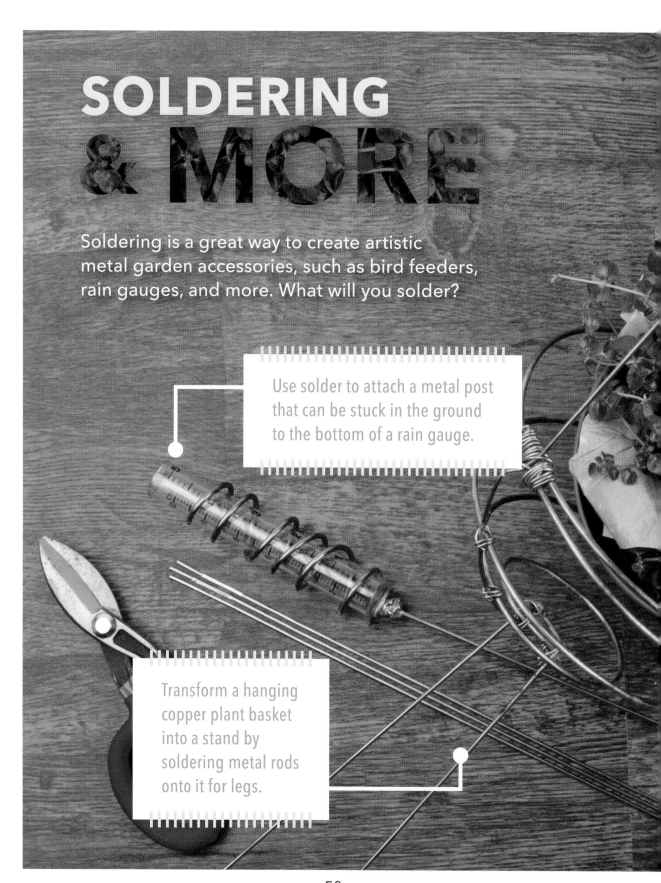

SOLDERING
& MORE

Soldering is a great way to create artistic metal garden accessories, such as bird feeders, rain gauges, and more. What will you solder?

Use solder to attach a metal post that can be stuck in the ground to the bottom of a rain gauge.

Transform a hanging copper plant basket into a stand by soldering metal rods onto it for legs.

UPCYCLING & MORE

Upcycle metal junk into something great! A little creativity goes a long way. What will you upcycle?

A tin can and some wire could become an outdoor lantern.

Cut up soda cans and turn them into flowers. Spray paint the flowers for a pop of color. The metal edges can be sharp, so be careful when handling the shapes.

Try cutting, sawing, and bending pieces of old silverware to make jewelry. Wear gloves and safety goggles when cutting or sawing silverware. And secure the silverware in a vise to help protect yourself from flying pieces.

WHAT NEXT?

Your metalworking project is a wrap. Now what? Don't pack away your supplies just yet! It's time to finish and style your hard work.

FINISHING TOUCHES

Examine your finished piece. Do you want to leave it as is to show the metal's natural color? Do you want to paint it or create a patina? What about adding decorations by using a stamp or an embossing stylus to etch patterns into the piece? Think about how you want to use what you made. Will you use it yourself, give it as a gift, or display it somewhere for people to admire? Will you photograph it to share on social media or maybe even sell it?

DISPLAYING PROJECTS

There are tons of ways to use and display metalworking projects. A metal lantern can be displayed on a desk or table indoors or hung outdoors. Metal sculptures can be placed on a shelf, mantel, or porch as decor. Jewelry can be worn or hung on wall pegs when not in use.

PHOTO STYLING TIPS

Follow these simple tips and tricks to make your projects pop!

- Keep your creations free from dust so they look their best.
- Choose a space that is well lit. Portable ring lights can be a great way to set up a photo studio wherever you are.
- Arrange your metalworking projects with items that relate to their look or function. But make sure the items don't overshadow the art!
- Choose a background that makes your project stand out.

BECOMING A METALWORKER

There are many paths to turning your love of metal into a career. Learning to work with metal can lead to jobs in mining, engineering, construction, welding, jewelry, art, and much more.

Many metalworkers get an education specifically to prepare for a career in metalworking. Some go to a college or trade school to study fine arts, engineering, or machine- and metalworking. There, they learn about the properties of metal and how to choose and use the correct tools to shape and create with it.

But not every metalworker gets a formal education. Some might learn the skills they need through apprenticeships or on-the-job training. Many others are self-taught. They may eventually turn a favorite hobby into a business by selling their creations online or in shops.

EL ANATSUI

El Anatsui is a Ghanaian sculptor known for creating large metal sculptures. Anatsui often uses found materials in his work. These include metal bottle caps, nails, and milk tins. Anatsui sometimes sews crushed metal pieces together with copper wire.

METAL ARTISTS AT WORK

Meet some artists who are moving and shaking in the metalworking world!

RICHARD SERRA

American artist Richard Serra crafts large abstract metal sculptures for urban spaces. Many of Serra's sculptures are focused on weight, balance, and gravity. Some of his outdoor installations are meant to change texture and color over time.

JEFF KOONS

Jeff Koons is an American artist known for incorporating pop culture and everyday objects into his art. Among Koons's most famous pieces are colorful mirror-plated stainless-steel sculptures that look like balloon animals.

TAMIKO KAWATA

Tamiko Kawata is a Japanese artist famous for her intricate safety pin artworks. By interlocking safety pins together, Kawata has created small sculptures and jewelry as well as large wall installations.

Forging is the technique used by blacksmiths to work iron and steel.

Drill presses allow metalworkers to drill holes in thick metal.

DO WHAT YOU LOVE!

Your project may be complete and your workshop cleaned up, but your metalworking journey is far from over! Think about the projects you made. How do they reflect your identity as an artist? What did you learn from them? What would you do differently next time? And what new techniques would you like to experiment with?

This book explored cutting, bending, soldering, upcycling, and finishing metal projects, but there are more metalworking techniques to discover. Forging is heating and hammering metal to form it into specific shapes. Reticulation is melting metal surfaces to create patterns and designs. And if you are able to find a class or program teaching metalworking that requires specialty machines, such as a bandsaw or drill press, there's no limit to what you can make! What new metalworking methods would you like to explore?

Metalworking is a fun and fulfilling hobby, but where else could your love of this craft take you? Maybe one day you'll make your own jewelry, start your own Etsy shop, or become a famous metal sculptor. So heat up your soldering iron, sharpen your tin snips, and gather your metals. Your imagination is the limit!

Reticulation is often used to add texture to pieces made with silver alloys.

61

GLOSSARY

apprenticeship—an arrangement in which a person learns a trade or a craft from a skilled worker.

audience—a group of readers, listeners, or spectators.

authentic—real or genuine.

casting—shaping a substance by pouring it into a mold and letting it harden.

concert—a musical performance or show.

decor—the style and layout of interior furnishings.

emboss—to decorate with a raised pattern or design.

engineering—the science of designing and building structures such as machines, cars, or roads.

etch—to make a pattern or design on a hard surface using either a sharp instrument or a substance that eats into the surface, such as acid. A combination of both methods may also be used.

geometric—made up of straight lines, circles, and other simple shapes.

graphic design—using type and images to arrange information or create an effect.

incorporating—including or working into.

installation—something put in place for use or viewing.

interlocking—joining or hooking together.

landform—a natural feature of the land, such as a hill or a river.

pandemic—an outbreak of a disease that spreads quickly throughout the world.

patina—a usually green film formed naturally on copper and bronze by long exposure or created artificially.

perspective–a particular attitude toward or way of looking at something.

scheme–an organized design.

spiral–a pattern that winds in a circle.

stylus–a pointed tool used to make marks in materials such as metal, wood, or clay.

technique–a method or style in which something is done.

tutorial–a lesson on how to do something. Tutorials are often presented through media such as videos or computer programs.

urban–of or relating to a city.

ventilated–exposed to fresh, freely moving air.

ONLINE RESOURCES

Booklinks
NONFICTION NETWORK
FREE! ONLINE NONFICTION RESOURCES

To learn more about metalworking, please visit **abdobooklinks.com** or scan this QR code. These links are routinely monitored and updated to provide the most current information available.

INDEX